MON1 CROSSWORD PUZZLES

© 2024

Across
1. A university town in Montana
3. Cold, slow-moving mass in a national park
4. Iconic American mammal
6. Western Montana's cultural hub

Down
1. Montana's nickname for its expansive skies
2. Famous national park with Old Faithful
5. Montana's capital

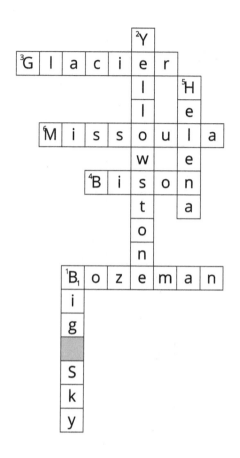

Across

1. A university town in Montana
3. Cold, slow-moving mass in a national park
4. Iconic American mammal
6. Western Montana's cultural hub

Down

1. Montana's nickname for its expansive skies
2. Famous national park with Old Faithful
5. Montana's capital

Across
1. Wide-open spaces for livestock
2. An accessory that keeps your trousers up
3. A precious gemstone, Montana's state gem
5. A dam on the Missouri River in Montana
6. Eroded terrain noted for its stark beauty

Down
4. Small water streams found in nature
7. A geographic area in Central Montana
8. A trailblazer or early settler

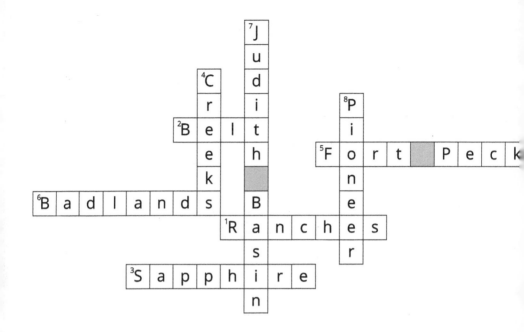

Across
1. Wide-open spaces for livestock
2. An accessory that keeps your trousers up
3. A precious gemstone, Montana's state gem
5. A dam on the Missouri River in Montana
6. Eroded terrain noted for its stark beauty

Down
4. Small water streams found in nature
7. A geographic area in Central Montana
8. A trailblazer or early settler

Across
2. A Montana town known for its ski resort
4. A variety of large North American fish
5. A community at the mouth of the Swan River
6. A town in northern Montana
7. Activity involving trails and natural terrains
8. The top of a mountain covered in snow

Down
1. A scenic national park with icy formations
3. A city in Montana with significant waterfalls

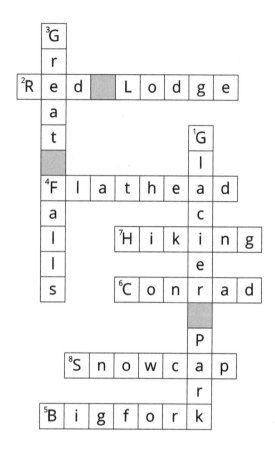

Across
2. A Montana town known for its ski resort
4. A variety of large North American fish
5. A community at the mouth of the Swan River
6. A town in northern Montana
7. Activity involving trails and natural terrains
8. The top of a mountain covered in snow

Down
1. A scenic national park with icy formations
3. A city in Montana with significant waterfalls

Across
1. A river and tribe in Idaho and Montana
2. A town in Rosebud County
3. Flat, open grassland
8. The river valley containing Bozeman and Big Sky

Down
4. A valley and river in western Montana
5. A county in north-central Montana
6. A town associated with energy production in Montana
7. A river and its associated mountain range in Montana

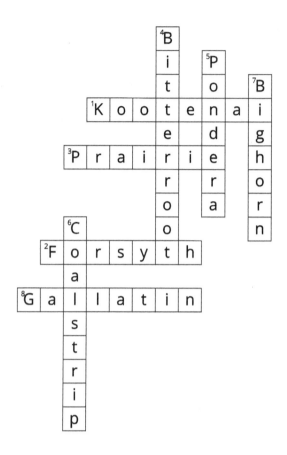

Across
1. A river and tribe in Idaho and Montana
2. A town in Rosebud County
3. Flat, open grassland
8. The river valley containing Bozeman and Big Sky

Down
4. A valley and river in western Montana
5. A county in north-central Montana
6. A town associated with energy production in Montana
7. A river and its associated mountain range in Montana

Across
1. Large antlered animal found in northern regions
4. A mountain range or pass explorer
5. Large North American bear
8. A city in northern Montana

Down
2. A city near Flathead Lake
3. A town in Beaverhead County
6. A small water stream named after a predator
7. A battle site associated with the Sioux

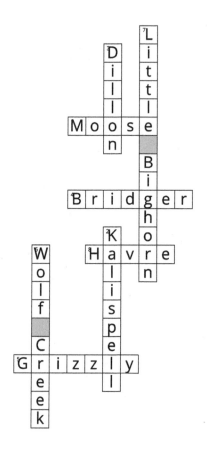

Across
1. Large antlered animal found in northern regions
4. A mountain range or pass explorer
5. Large North American bear
8. A city in northern Montana

Down
2. A city near Flathead Lake
3. A town in Beaverhead County
6. A small water stream named after a predator
7. A battle site associated with the Sioux

Across
1. A town in northeastern Montana
5. Livestock found on farms
7. The largest city in Montana

Down
2. A town in Jefferson County
3. A gathering featuring Native American dancing and music
4. Winter sport involving descending slopes
6. A mountain range in southern Montana

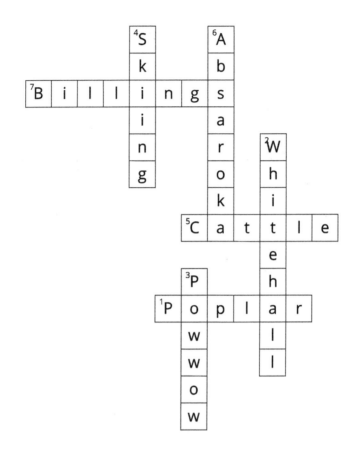

Across
1. A town in northeastern Montana
5. Livestock found on farms
7. The largest city in Montana

Down
2. A town in Jefferson County
3. A gathering featuring Native American dancing and music
4. Winter sport involving descending slopes
6. A mountain range in southern Montana

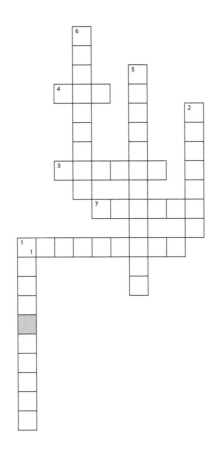

Across
1. A popular ski resort town in Montana
3. A classic Western character with a hat and boots
4. Large deer species in North America
7. A deep red gemstone, also Montana's state gem

Down
1. A town in northeastern Montana
2. A scenic reservoir south of Bozeman
5. Winter sport on a board
6. A small Montana town with railway history

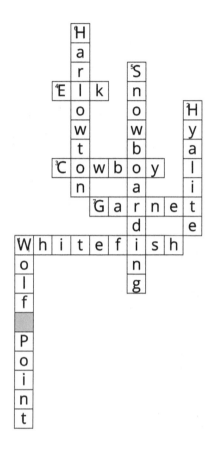

Across
1. A popular ski resort town in Montana
3. A classic Western character with a hat and boots
4. Large deer species in North America
7. A deep red gemstone, also Montana's state gem

Down
1. A town in northeastern Montana
2. A scenic reservoir south of Bozeman
5. Winter sport on a board
6. A small Montana town with railway history

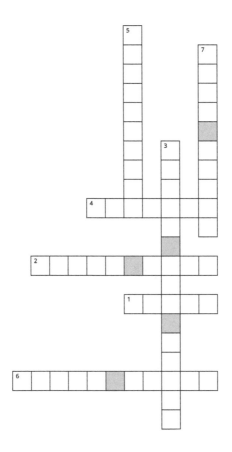

Across

1. A competitive event featuring bronco and bull riding
2. A lake formed by an earthquake in Montana
4. The pursuit of wild game as a sport
5. A type of herb and a county in Montana

Down

3. Famous explorers of the American West
6. A community west of Missoula with French heritage
7. A city known for its historic prison

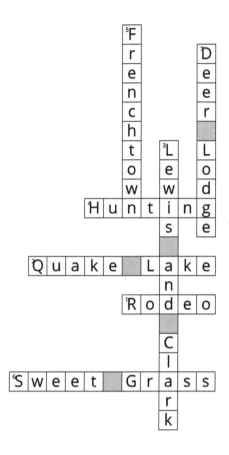

Across
1. A competitive event featuring bronco and bull riding
2. A lake formed by an earthquake in Montana
4. The pursuit of wild game as a sport
6. A type of herb and a county in Montana

Down
3. Famous explorers of the American West
5. A community west of Missoula with French heritage
7. A city known for its historic prison

Across
2. The process of gathering ripe crops
3. A town in Granite County known for its ranching
4. A mining city known for its rich history and large hill
5. A city on the southern shore of Flathead Lake
6. A town known for high winds and a steep drop

Down
1. A town known for its coal power plant
4. A town in southeastern Montana
7. A piece of land granted for farming

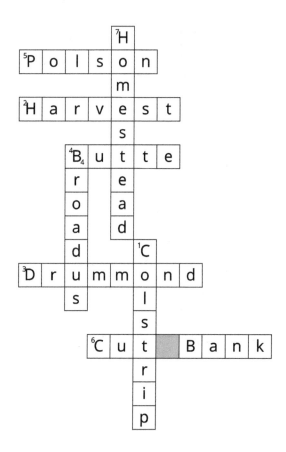

Across
2. The process of gathering ripe crops
3. A town in Granite County known for its ranching
4. A mining city known for its rich history and large hill
5. A city on the southern shore of Flathead Lake
6. A town known for high winds and a steep drop

Down
1. A town known for its coal power plant
4. A town in southeastern Montana
7. A piece of land granted for farming

Across

1. A sport involving catching fish with a rod and artificial flies
4. A place to stay in the wilderness or a small hotel
5. A Native American tribe in Montana
7. A county in the Bitterroot Valley

Down

2. A town along the Yellowstone River, gateway to the park
3. A scenic area in southwestern Montana
6. A mountain range known for its unique minerals
8. A popular fish for anglers in Montana's streams

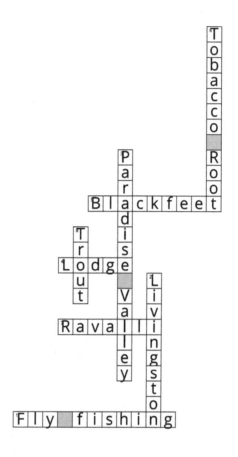

Across
1. A sport involving catching fish with a rod and artificial flies
4. A place to stay in the wilderness or a small hotel
5. A Native American tribe in Montana
7. A county in the Bitterroot Valley

Down
2. A town along the Yellowstone River, gateway to the park
3. A scenic area in southwestern Montana
6. A mountain range known for its unique minerals
8. A popular fish for anglers in Montana's streams

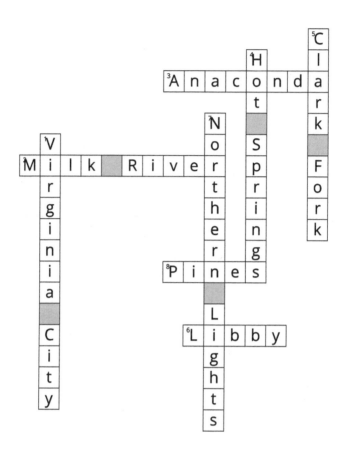

Across
2. A river flowing through northeastern Montana
3. A town known for its smelter stack
6. A town in northwest Montana near the Cabinet Mountains
8. Evergreen trees commonly found in cold climates

Down
1. A historic town known for its role in the gold rush
4. Natural thermal pools
5. A major river in Montana
7. A vibrant display in the Arctic sky

Across
1. A small town known for its nearby fishing and hunting
4. A town known for its historic dinosaur findings
5. A city at the confluence of three rivers
7. A purple variety of quartz, found in certain Montana mountains

Down
2. The act of extracting valuable minerals from the earth
3. Untouched natural areas away from civilization
4. A Native American tribe known in Montana
6. A rural valley in southwestern Montana

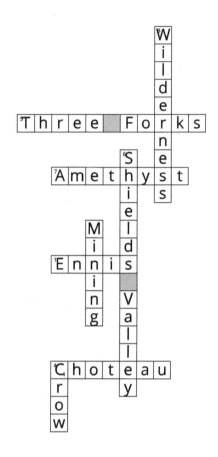

Across
1. A small town known for its nearby fishing and hunting
4. A town known for its historic dinosaur findings
5. A city at the confluence of three rivers
7. A purple variety of quartz, found in certain Montana mountains

Down
2. The act of extracting valuable minerals from the earth
3. Untouched natural areas away from civilization
4. A Native American tribe known in Montana
6. A rural valley in southwestern Montana

Across
2. The past tense of 'can', indicating past ability or possibility.
3. To compose text
5. Seat with a back, typically for one person
6. Even though or although
8. Remains of a destroyed or sunken ship

Down
1. A major mountain range spanning the western North America
4. Opposite of victory
7. Sport involving physical exercises and performances

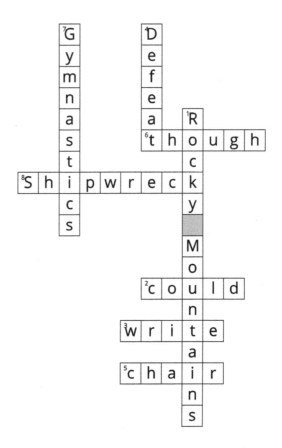

Across
2. The past tense of 'can', indicating past ability or possibility.
3. To compose text
5. Seat with a back, typically for one person
6. Even though or although
8. Remains of a destroyed or sunken ship

Down
1. A major mountain range spanning the western North America
4. Opposite of victory
7. Sport involving physical exercises and performances

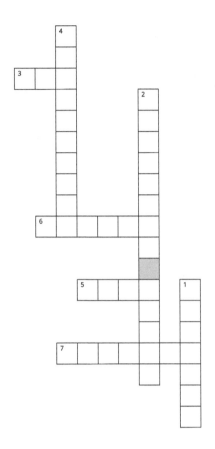

Across
3. Flying mammal or sports equipment
5. Originating from a certain place
6. Leafy green vegetable, slightly bitter
7. Diverse or assorted

Down
1. A communicated note or information
2. Sweet, pale green fruit
4. Large green fruit with watery flesh

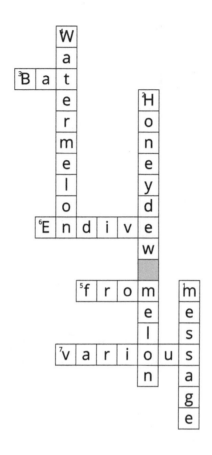

Across
3. Flying mammal or sports equipment
5. Originating from a certain place
6. Leafy green vegetable, slightly bitter
7. Diverse or assorted

Down
1. A communicated note or information
2. Sweet, pale green fruit
4. Large green fruit with watery flesh

Across

1. Law enforcement officers.
2. A measure of the speed or frequency of occurrence of something.
4. Ground or territory
5. Defeat or deprivation

Down

1. A specific location or arrangement
3. Ocean floor

Across
1. Law enforcement officers.
2. A measure of the speed or frequency of occurrence of something.
4. Ground or territory
5. Defeat or deprivation

Down
1. A specific location or arrangement
3. Ocean floor

Across
1. Think about carefully
3. The season following winter
5. Competent or capable
8. Sandy shore

Down
2. Cooking by dry heat in an oven
4. Essential or required
6. A bulbous vegetable known for its crisp texture and mild flavor
7. Pungent vegetable used in cooking

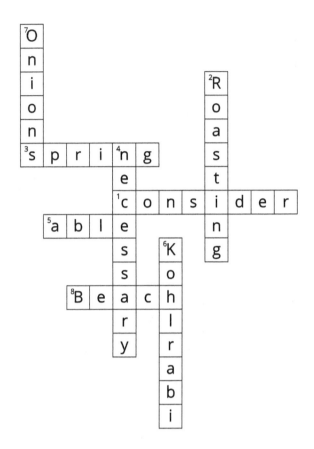

Across
1. Think about carefully
3. The season following winter
5. Competent or capable
8. Sandy shore

Down
2. Cooking by dry heat in an oven
4. Essential or required
6. A bulbous vegetable known for its crisp texture and mild flavor
7. Pungent vegetable used in cooking

Across
4. In a short time or shortly.
5. breaking of waves on the shore
6. Area or district
7. Belonging to whom?

Down
1. Previous or prior in time, order, or position.
2. Moving to a surface or position
3. Firearm
8. Something you might lend or shake

Across
4. In a short time or shortly.
5. breaking of waves on the shore
6. Area or district
7. Belonging to whom?

Down
1. Previous or prior in time, order, or position.
2. Moving to a surface or position
3. Firearm
8. Something you might lend or shake

Across
2. Place to sit, or a right to be in a particular place
4. Direction opposite to north.
5. A ring-shaped coral reef, island, or series of islets surrounding a lagoon.
6. One of two choices or possibilities

Down
1. Substance used to enhance taste
3. Possibly or might be
7. Visual representation or image
8. Fishing boat designed for large catches

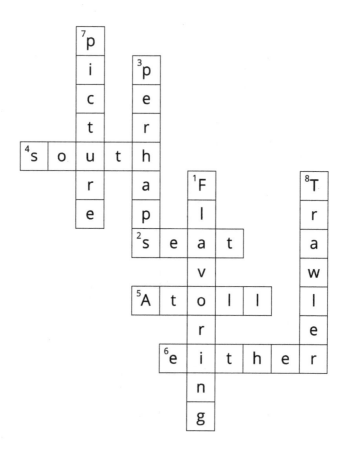

Across
2. Place to sit, or a right to be in a particular place
4. Direction opposite to north.
5. A ring-shaped coral reef, island, or series of islets surrounding a lagoon.
6. One of two choices or possibilities

Down
1. Substance used to enhance taste
3. Possibly or might be
7. Visual representation or image
8. Fishing boat designed for large catches

Across
3. Lying in the sun to tan the skin
5. Medical professional
6. Single side of a sheet of paper in a book
7. Staple grain grown in ears on tall grass

Down
1. Container for baking individual muffins
2. Room or area for cooking
4. Softening meat before cooking

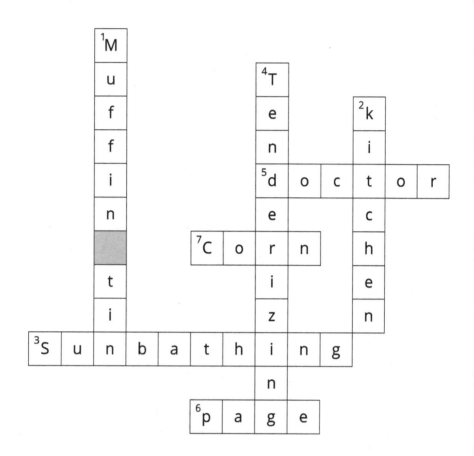

Across
3. Lying in the sun to tan the skin
5. Medical professional
6. Single side of a sheet of paper in a book
7. Staple grain grown in ears on tall grass

Down
1. Container for baking individual muffins
2. Room or area for cooking
4. Softening meat before cooking

Across

4. Specific or detailed
5. Material for writing or printing
7. Sufficient or as much as needed
8. Protection or safety measures

Down

1. Tower emitting light for navigational guidance
2. Relating to government or public affairs.
3. Moving from one side to another.
5. Springing off the ground

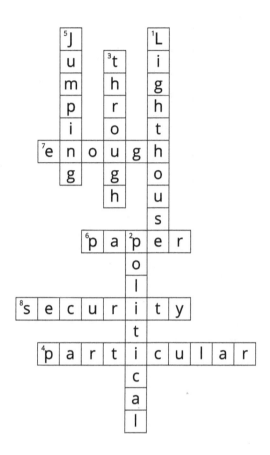

Across
4. Specific or detailed
6. Material for writing or printing
7. Sufficient or as much as needed
8. Protection or safety measures

Down
1. Tower emitting light for navigational guidance
2. Relating to government or public affairs.
3. Moving from one side to another.
5. Springing off the ground

Across

2. Rule violation involving position in some sports
3. Shape or structure
4. One of two equal parts
7. A planned task or endeavor, especially in business or science

Down

1. Introduction of a new element or quality into something
4. Perceive by ear
5. Reflexive form of pronoun 'he', indicating he is performing an action
6. Plan of action for achieving a goal

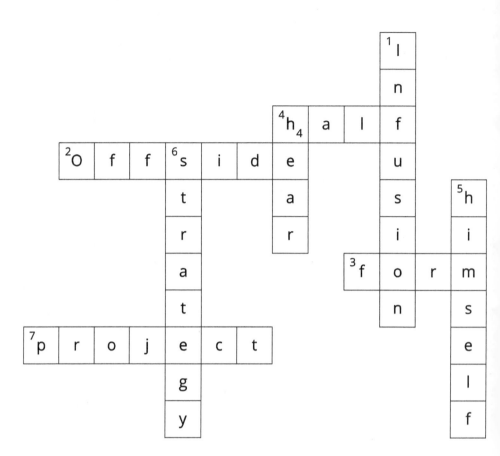

Across
2. Rule violation involving position in some sports
3. Shape or structure
4. One of two equal parts
7. A planned task or endeavor, especially in business or science

Down
1. Introduction of a new element or quality into something
4. Perceive by ear
5. Reflexive form of pronoun 'he', indicating he is performing an action
6. Plan of action for achieving a goal

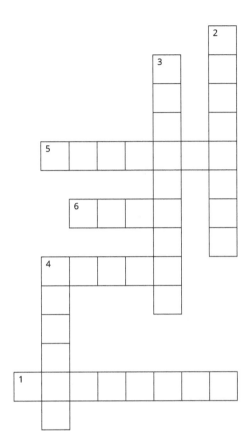

Across
1. Aquatic mammals known for their intelligence
4. Significant or principal
5. Mirror or show an image again
6. Continuous mark or boundary

Down
2. Art of creating images using colors
3. Small, round berry, typically dark blue
4. Systematic procedure

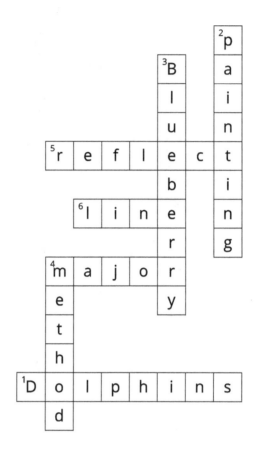

Across
1. Aquatic mammals known for their intelligence
4. Significant or principal
5. Mirror or show an image again
6. Continuous mark or boundary

Down
2. Art of creating images using colors
3. Small, round berry, typically dark blue
4. Systematic procedure

Across
1. Feel curiosity or amazement
2. In association with each other
4. Vertical structure that encloses or divides an area
5. Edible shoots known for their distinct flavor
8. The central point or position.

Down
3. Type of lettuce with long, sturdy leaves
6. Commonly or as a rule
7. Tart red berry often used in sauces and juices

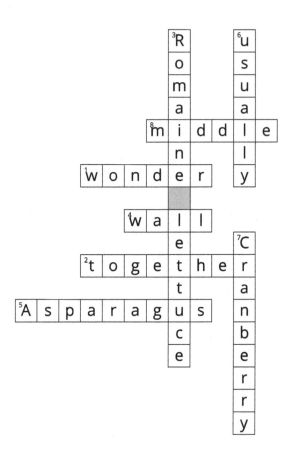

Across
1. Feel curiosity or amazement
2. In association with each other
4. Vertical structure that encloses or divides an area
5. Edible shoots known for their distinct flavor
8. The central point or position.

Down
3. Type of lettuce with long, sturdy leaves
6. Commonly or as a rule
7. Tart red berry often used in sauces and juices

Across
1. Identify or label
2. Peppery, leafy green
3. Tropical trees known for their large, fan-like leaves
7. To be anxious or concerned

Down
4. A series of actions conducted to achieve a result
5. Following the old ways
6. Relating to one's private life
8. Official documentation or highest score

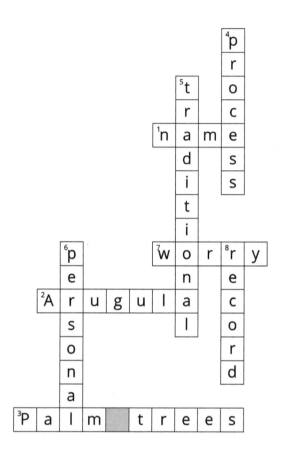

Across
1. Identify or label
2. Peppery, leafy green
3. Tropical trees known for their large, fan-like leaves
7. To be anxious or concerned

Down
4. A series of actions conducted to achieve a result
5. Following the old ways
6. Relating to one's private life
8. Official documentation or highest score

Across
3. Starchy tuberous vegetables.
4. Not heavy or having high intensity in terms of weight or illumination
5. Possess or own something
7. Area designated for the game involving clubs and balls

Down
1. Large venue for watching football games
2. Process of choosing leaders
6. Person trained in sports and physical exercise
8. Issue or difficulty needing resolution

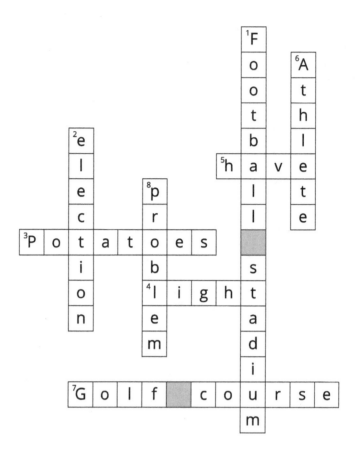

Across

3. Starchy tuberous vegetables.
4. Not heavy or having high intensity in terms of weight or illumination
5. Possess or own something
7. Area designated for the game involving clubs and balls

Down

1. Large venue for watching football games
2. Process of choosing leaders
6. Person trained in sports and physical exercise
8. Issue or difficulty needing resolution

Across
2. Standard clothing worn by members of a group.
3. Force exerted on an object.
4. Organization or heavy instrument for hitting
6. Green vegetable often found in trees

Down
1. Person who saves swimmers in danger
5. Point of debate or query
7. Removing the outer layer from fruits or vegetables

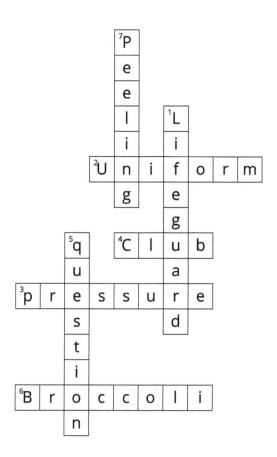

Across
2. Standard clothing worn by members of a group.
3. Force exerted on an object.
4. Organization or heavy instrument for hitting
6. Green vegetable often found in trees

Down
1. Person who saves swimmers in danger
5. Point of debate or query
7. Removing the outer layer from fruits or vegetables

Across
1. Not old; having lived or existed for only a short time.
3. State of tranquility or freedom from conflict
4. Financial institution or river edge
6. A set of connected things or parts forming a complex whole.

Down
2. Item of furniture with flat top
5. Act of replacing one thing with another
7. Korean martial art focused on kicks and punches
8. Sport or activity of riding bicycles

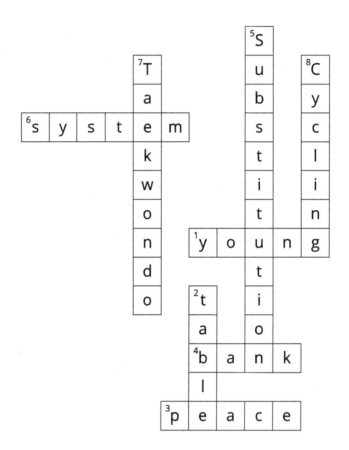

Across
1. Not old; having lived or existed for only a short time.
3. State of tranquility or freedom from conflict
4. Financial institution or river edge
6. A set of connected things or parts forming a complex whole.

Down
2. Item of furniture with flat top
5. Act of replacing one thing with another
7. Korean martial art focused on kicks and punches
8. Sport or activity of riding bicycles

Across
1. Series or sequence of items
2. To blend until smooth, often with oil and vinegar
6. A business entity or association
7. Sport involving swords and protective gear
8. Liquid made by boiling bones or vegetables

Down
3. Cooking technique involving brief boiling followed by ice water
4. Total or sum
5. Success or conquest in competition

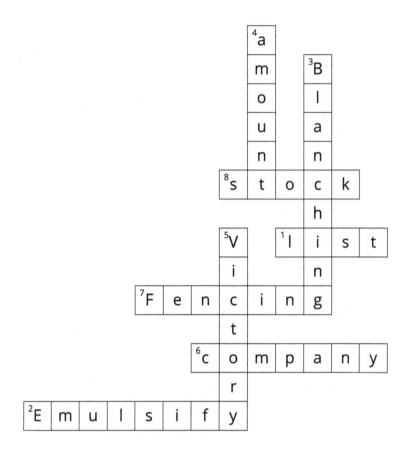

Across
1. Series or sequence of items
2. To blend until smooth, often with oil and vinegar
6. A business entity or association
7. Sport involving swords and protective gear
8. Liquid made by boiling bones or vegetables

Down
3. Cooking technique involving brief boiling followed by ice water
4. Total or sum
5. Success or conquest in competition

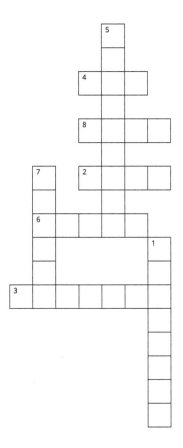

Across
2. Intense and destructive burning
3. Disc used in recreational games.
4. Of poor quality or unfavorable
5. Essential for life, covers 71% of Earth's surface
8. At that time or afterwards

Down
1. Salad component or condiment
6. Located next to the sea
7. Legal professional

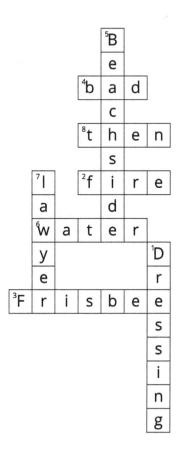

Across
2. Intense and destructive burning
3. Disc used in recreational games.
4. Of poor quality or unfavorable
6. Essential for life, covers 71% of Earth's surface
8. At that time or afterwards

Down
1. Salad component or condiment
5. Located next to the sea
7. Legal professional

Across
3. Seafood, small and decapod crustaceans
4. Number following nine
6. An ancient throwing sport in track and field
8. Seat for riding horses

Down
1. Small, onion-like herb
2. Six zeros figure
5. Provide medical care or enjoyment
7. Very young child

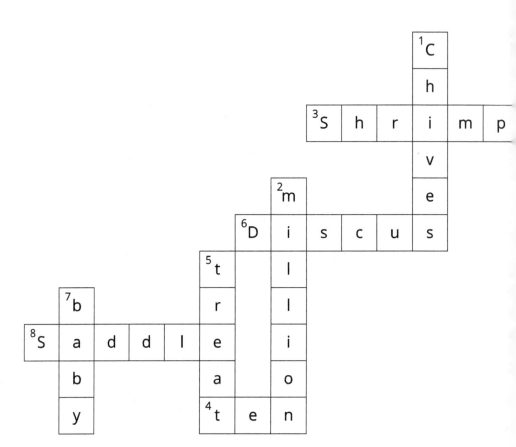

Across
3. Seafood, small and decapod crustaceans
4. Number following nine
6. An ancient throwing sport in track and field
8. Seat for riding horses

Down
1. Small, onion-like herb
2. Six zeros figure
5. Provide medical care or enjoyment
7. Very young child

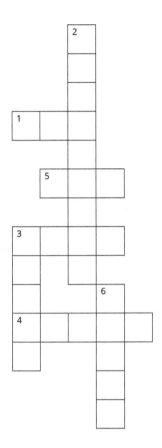

Across
1. Mesh used in sports or fishing
3. At what time or on what occasion.
4. Conceal or include a protective layer
5. Armed conflict between countries

Down
2. Type of ecosystem found in oceans
3. Observe or keep under close watch
6. Edible root vegetables known for their deep red color

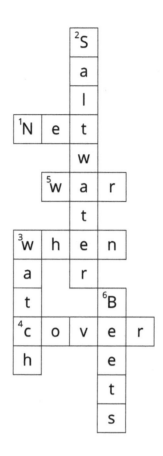

Across
1. Mesh used in sports or fishing
3. At what time or on what occasion.
4. Conceal or include a protective layer
5. Armed conflict between countries

Down
2. Type of ecosystem found in oceans
3. Observe or keep under close watch
6. Edible root vegetables known for their deep red color

Across
1. Appliance for cooking food by heat
3. Be aware of through experience or information
4. A length or portion of time
5. Secure and protected.
7. Recreational activity involving a parachute pulled by a boat

Down
2. Truly or indeed
5. Fruit related to apples and pears
8. Small green vegetables resembling miniature cabbages

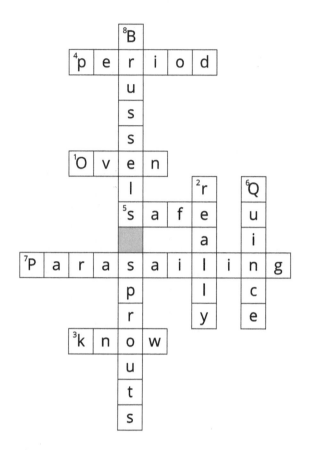

Across
1. Appliance for cooking food by heat
3. Be aware of through experience or information
4. A length or portion of time
5. Secure and protected.
7. Recreational activity involving a parachute pulled by a boat

Down
2. Truly or indeed
6. Fruit related to apples and pears
8. Small green vegetables resembling miniature cabbages

Across
2. Demonstrative pronoun for indicating specific things
3. Worth or significance
4. Action or process of doing something.
5. Flightless bird with brown fuzzy skin

Down
1. Sport with ball and bat played primarily in Commonwealth countries
6. Apparatus for performing tasks
7. Having achieved a goal or recognition

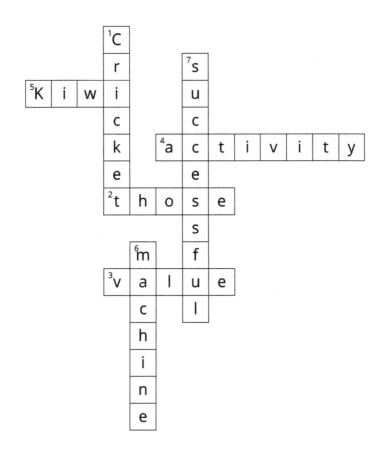

Across
2. Demonstrative pronoun for indicating specific things
3. Worth or significance
4. Action or process of doing something.
5. Flightless bird with brown fuzzy skin

Down
1. Sport with ball and bat played primarily in Commonwealth countries
6. Apparatus for performing tasks
7. Having achieved a goal or recognition

Across
3. The upper part of the body or an organization
4. Broad in extent
5. Each of the digits of the hand
6. Declaration or assertion.

Down
1. Leafy greens with a pungent flavor often used in cooking.
2. To instruct or give knowledge to someone
7. Educator at a higher learning institution.
8. Specific task or duty assigned to a person or group

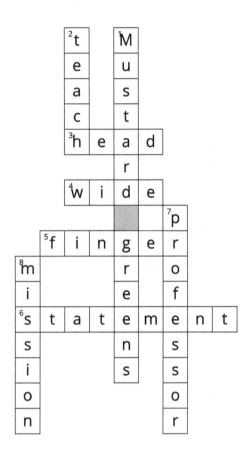

Across
3. The upper part of the body or an organization
4. Broad in extent
5. Each of the digits of the hand
6. Declaration or assertion.

Down
1. Leafy greens with a pungent flavor often used in cooking.
2. To instruct or give knowledge to someone
7. Educator at a higher learning institution.
8. Specific task or duty assigned to a person or group

Across
2. To propel something through the air with force.
3. Rank or position following second
4. Edibles prepared and consumed
6. A collection of items that belong together or are used together.

Down
1. Quite or reasonably
5. Long-distance running event
7. Flowing or contemporary

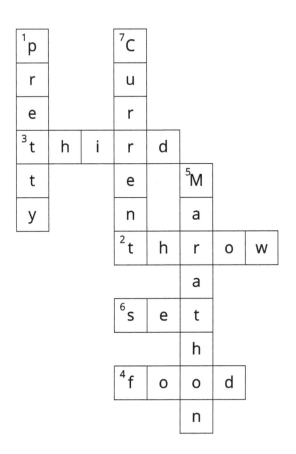

Across
2. To propel something through the air with force.
3. Rank or position following second
4. Edibles prepared and consumed
6. A collection of items that belong together or are used together.

Down
1. Quite or reasonably
5. Long-distance running event
7. Flowing or contemporary

Across
1. Fail to remember
5. Final in a series
6. To hold or include within
8. Coastal area with sand or pebbles

Down
2. Manner or mode of expression.
3. Pertaining to; concerning
4. Citrus fruit known for its color and taste
7. Cooking food over direct heat

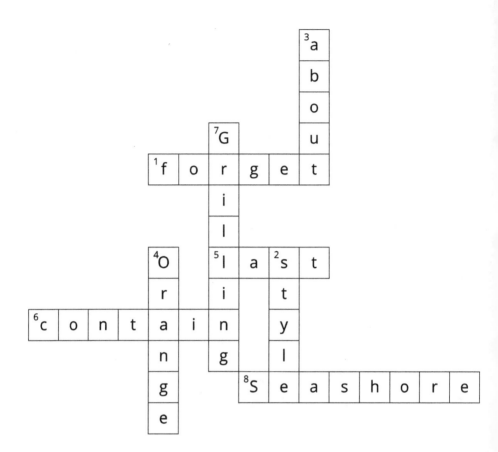

Across
1. Fail to remember
5. Final in a series
6. To hold or include within
8. Coastal area with sand or pebbles

Down
2. Manner or mode of expression.
3. Pertaining to; concerning
4. Citrus fruit known for its color and taste
7. Cooking food over direct heat

Across
1. Container for carrying items
3. To contain as a part of something
5. Hitting in baseball
6. Not long past

Down
2. Team sport played with a ball on a rectangular court
4. Periodical publication with articles and pictures
7. Army member or warrior
8. Large ocean wave caused by underwater seismic activity

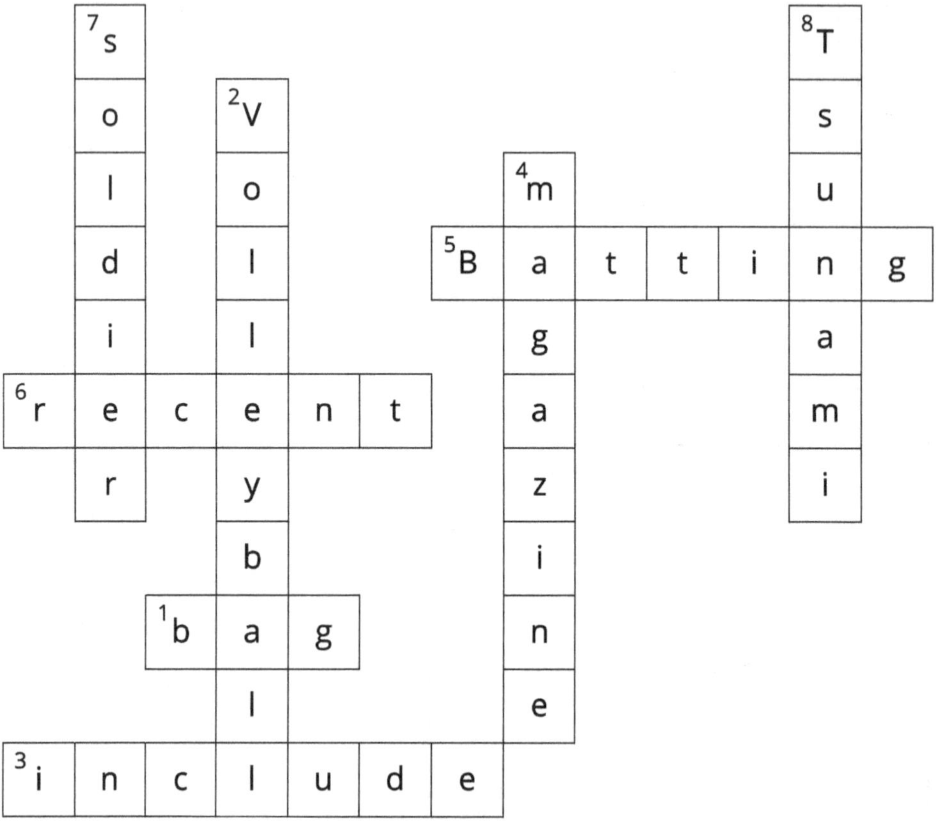
7 soldier
2 Volleyball
4 magazine
8 Tsunami
5 Batting
6 recent
1 bag
3 include

Across
1. Container for carrying items
3. To contain as a part of something
5. Hitting in baseball
6. Not long past

Down
2. Team sport played with a ball on a rectangular court
4. Periodical publication with articles and pictures
7. Army member or warrior
8. Large ocean wave caused by underwater seismic activity

Across
1. Related to cooking or the kitchen
2. To extend or stretch out an arm
6. To connect or find common ground
7. Catch wind for movement
8. Drinking vessel or a trophy in sports

Down
3. Smartphone feature with edible name
4. Set of cooking instructions
5. Primary or chief

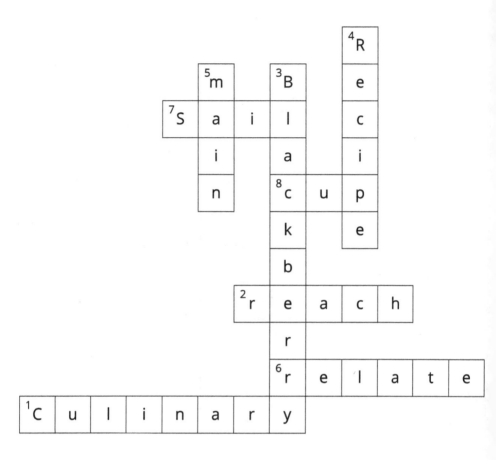

Across
1. Related to cooking or the kitchen
2. To extend or stretch out an arm
6. To connect or find common ground
7. Catch wind for movement
8. Drinking vessel or a trophy in sports

Down
3. Smartphone feature with edible name
4. Set of cooking instructions
5. Primary or chief

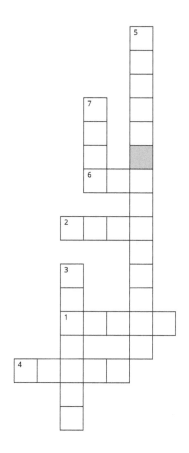

Across
1. Rise to an upright position
2. Come into the presence or company of someone
4. A series of thoughts during sleep or a cherished aspiration
6. Recently developed or introduced

Down
3. As a substitute or alternative
5. Activity of observing large marine mammals at sea
7. Scheme or strategy for achieving an objective

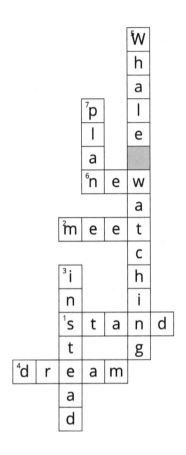

Across
1. Rise to an upright position
2. Come into the presence or company of someone
4. A series of thoughts during sleep or a cherished aspiration
6. Recently developed or introduced

Down
3. As a substitute or alternative
5. Activity of observing large marine mammals at sea
7. Scheme or strategy for achieving an objective

Across
2. Flowing naturally or in business or finance
3. Narrative or account of events
4. Extremely large in size
5. Tally or record in games
7. Aromatic bulb used in cooking

Down
1. Vibrantly colored fruit with spikey appearance
3. Expanse or a vast vacuum outside the Earth's atmosphere
6. Root vegetable, similar to a large turnip

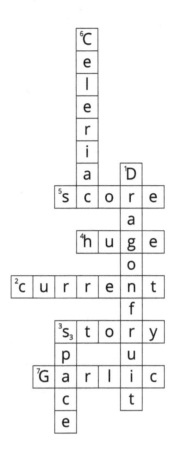

Across
2. Flowing naturally or in business or finance
3. Narrative or account of events
4. Extremely large in size
5. Tally or record in games
7. Aromatic bulb used in cooking

Down
1. Vibrantly colored fruit with spikey appearance
3. Expanse or a vast vacuum outside the Earth's atmosphere
6. Root vegetable, similar to a large turnip

Across
2. Object of effort or ambition
4. System or group of connected people or things
5. Coastal water body where river meets sea
7. Speed competition

Down
1. Facts or data provided about a particular topic.
3. Detailed examination or evaluation
6. Minimal or the smallest in amount
8. Structure built to protect against waves

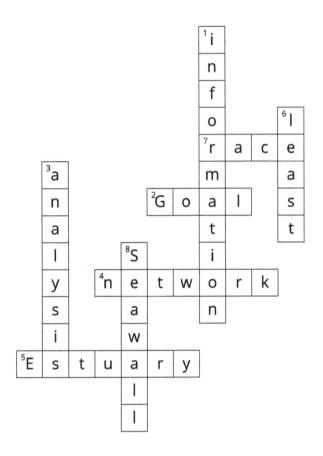

Across
2. Object of effort or ambition
4. System or group of connected people or things
5. Coastal water body where river meets sea
7. Speed competition

Down
1. Facts or data provided about a particular topic.
3. Detailed examination or evaluation
6. Minimal or the smallest in amount
8. Structure built to protect against waves

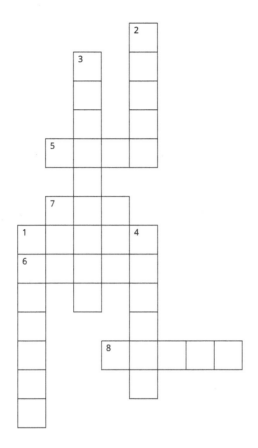

Across
5. At a distance or from this place
6. A number between seven and nine
7. For each or according to
8. Group of students or a division of study

Down
1. Official who enforces the rules in sports
2. Medium of exchange and economic transaction
3. Information or awareness
4. Refers to itself

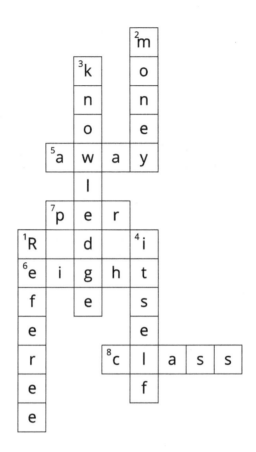

Across
5. At a distance or from this place
6. A number between seven and nine
7. For each or according to
8. Group of students or a division of study

Down
1. Official who enforces the rules in sports
2. Medium of exchange and economic transaction
3. Information or awareness
4. Refers to itself

Across
1. Occurring frequently or widespread
2. System of communication through speech
3. Contribute or incorporate
8. large body of people united by common descent, culture, or language

Down
4. Playing area specifically designed for basketball
5. Segment of play in baseball
6. One who oversees employees or operations
7. A type of citrus fruit known for its rough, unsightly skin

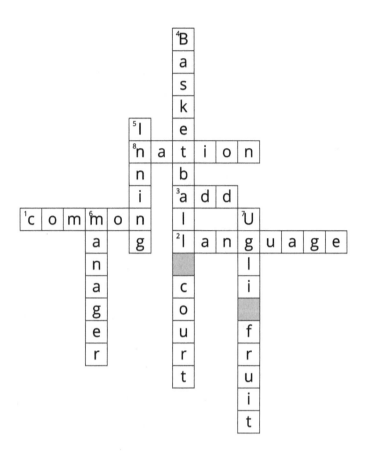

Across
1. Occurring frequently or widespread
2. System of communication through speech
3. Contribute or incorporate
8. large body of people united by common descent, culture, or language

Down
4. Playing area specifically designed for basketball
5. Segment of play in baseball
6. One who oversees employees or operations
7. A type of citrus fruit known for its rough, unsightly skin

Across
1. Cutting food into small cubes
2. Activity of navigating watercraft
5. Sketch or tie in competition
7. Seaweed used in sushi
8. Guard from harm or danger

Down
3. Process of turning sugar brown
4. Place where transportation vehicles stop for passengers or goods.
6. Expression emphasizing truth

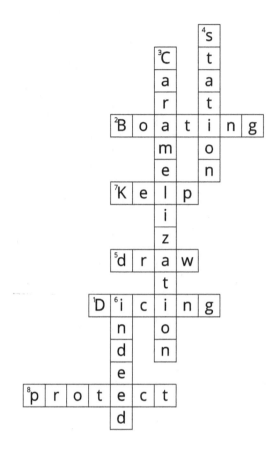

Across
1. Cutting food into small cubes
2. Activity of navigating watercraft
5. Sketch or tie in competition
7. Seaweed used in sushi
8. Guard from harm or danger

Down
3. Process of turning sugar brown
4. Place where transportation vehicles stop for passengers or goods.
6. Expression emphasizing truth

Across
3. Take away or eliminate
4. The action of working dough with hands
5. Fruit known for its round shape and crisp taste
7. Adult female

Down
1. Scheduled series of events or activities
2. Large, fast-swimming oceanic fish
3. Way in which two or more people are connected
6. Act of cutting food into pieces

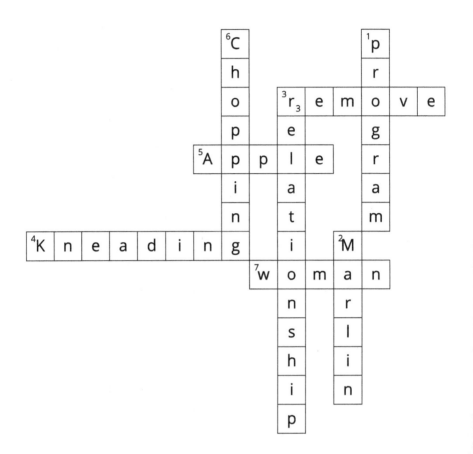

Across
3. Take away or eliminate
4. The action of working dough with hands
5. Fruit known for its round shape and crisp taste
7. Adult female

Down
1. Scheduled series of events or activities
2. Large, fast-swimming oceanic fish
3. Way in which two or more people are connected
6. Act of cutting food into pieces

Across
2. Spear-like implement thrown in sports
3. Large aquatic mammals
7. One who plays games or sports
8. Spherical object used in games

Down
1. Reflexive form of "they"
4. Small, crisp, often spicy root vegetables
5. Ten times ten
6. Nevertheless or but

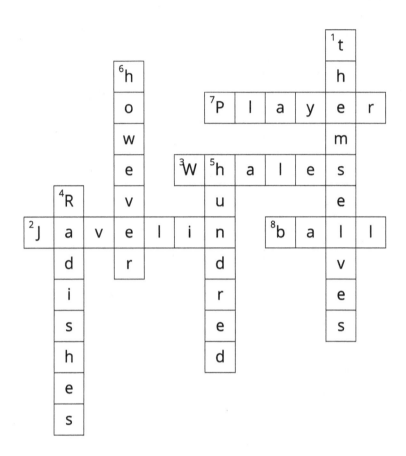

Across
2. Spear-like implement thrown in sports
3. Large aquatic mammals
7. One who plays games or sports
8. Spherical object used in games

Down
1. Reflexive form of "they"
4. Small, crisp, often spicy root vegetables
5. Ten times ten
6. Nevertheless or but

Across
1. Individual part of a group
2. Break in a sports game for rest and strategies
4. Cease to live
5. A type of squash that grows long and green
6. Sport involving gloves and rings

Down
3. The playing field for a popular American sport
7. Central organ of the circulatory system
8. Form of exercise involving rapid movement on foot.

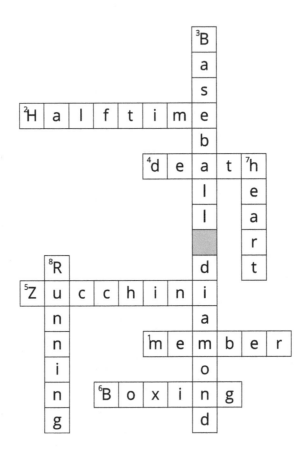

Across
1. Individual part of a group
2. Break in a sports game for rest and strategies
4. Cease to live
5. A type of squash that grows long and green
6. Sport involving gloves and rings

Down
3. The playing field for a popular American sport
7. Central organ of the circulatory system
8. Form of exercise involving rapid movement on foot.

Across
1. However; nevertheless
3. Exceptional or noteworthy
4. Direction opposite of east
6. Older or high-ranking person
7. Resolution or choice made after consideration

Down
2. Leafy green vegetable, similar to beet greens
5. Occurring abruptly or unexpectedly
8. Indicating an unspecified number in a group

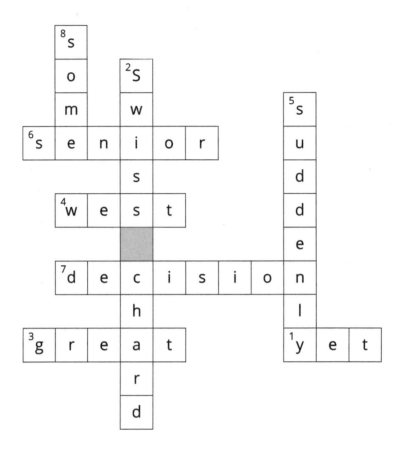

Across
1. However; nevertheless
3. Exceptional or noteworthy
4. Direction opposite of east
6. Older or high-ranking person
7. Resolution or choice made after consideration

Down
2. Leafy green vegetable, similar to beet greens
5. Occurring abruptly or unexpectedly
8. Indicating an unspecified number in a group

Across
1. Difficult or challenging
3. Enclosed space in a building
4. To halt or cease movement
7. Sport involving wind-propelled boats

Down
2. Aquatic plant used in salads
5. Activity of moving through water by body movement
6. Not high or above average in height or amount

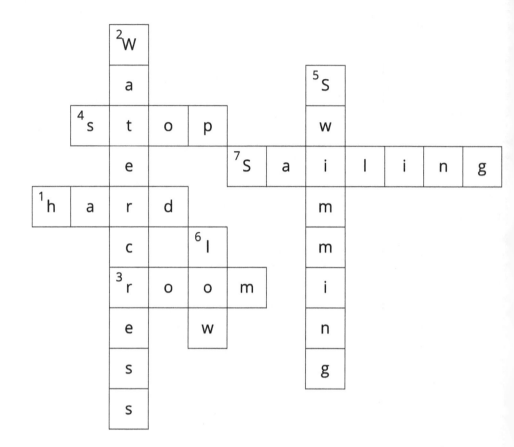

Across
1. Difficult or challenging
3. Enclosed space in a building
4. To halt or cease movement
7. Sport involving wind-propelled boats

Down
2. Aquatic plant used in salads
5. Activity of moving through water by body movement
6. Not high or above average in height or amount

Across
3. Close by
5. The Earth or society at large
6. Elevated or lofty
8. Express in words

Down
1. Free from obstruction or easily understood
2. Long, green, crisp vegetable
4. Temperature at which liquid turns to vapor
7. Lower surface of a room

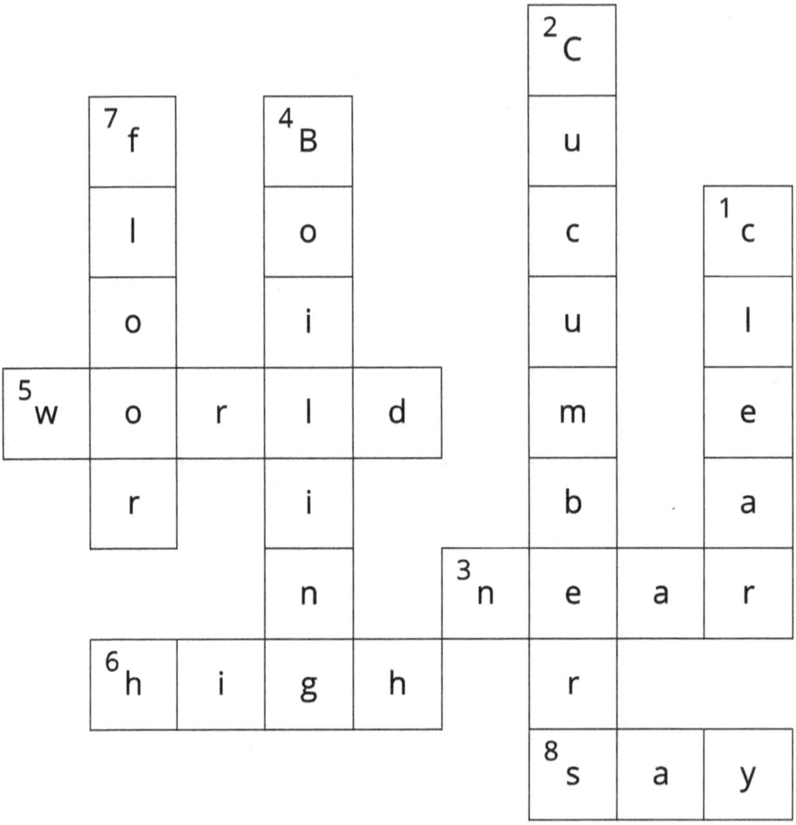

Crossword

Grid letters (as filled):

- 2 Down: c, u, c, u, m, b, e, r
- 7 Down: f, l, o, o, r
- 4 Down: B, o, i, l, i, n, g
- 1 Down: c, l, e, a, r
- 5 Across: w, o, r, l, d
- 3 Across: n, e, a, r
- 6 Across: h, i, g, h
- 8 Across: s, a, y

Across
3. Close by
5. The Earth or society at large
6. Elevated or lofty
8. Express in words

Down
1. Free from obstruction or easily understood
2. Long, green, crisp vegetable
4. Temperature at which liquid turns to vapor
7. Lower surface of a room

Made in United States
Troutdale, OR
12/22/2024

27177425R00060